Are You Good Enough Yet?

A BOOK FOR
PERFECTIONISTS
and all who try too hard
or worry too much

Fr. Joe Kempf

TWENTY-THIRD PUBLICATIONS

twentythirdpublications.com

Twenty-Third Publications
977 Hartford Turnpike Unit A
Waterford, CT 06385
(860) 437-3012 or (800) 321-0411
www.twentythirdpublications.com

Cover photo: MarekPhotoDesign.com / stock.adobe.com

ISBN: 978-1-62785-797-0
Printed in the U.S.A.

 A division of Bayard, Inc.

CONTENTS

Appendices

INTRODUCTION

You try so hard, don't you? Isn't it exhausting sometimes? Wouldn't it be great to live without that anxious pit in your stomach—to have a sense of peace and safety instead of feeling like there is always more you must do, more people to please, more arenas where you must prove yourself?

If you sometimes feel this way, the seeds of that struggle may have been planted in your childhood or adolescence. It could be, for example, that you heard words growing up that led you to feel you weren't good enough, that it wasn't safe for you to just be yourself. Or maybe there were messages you *didn't* hear that would have helped you better believe in yourself. Whatever the cause, I'm so sorry for whatever you suffered that kept you from knowing deep down that you are already enough, just as you are; that it is not your responsibility to fix everything; that you have nothing to prove, nothing to earn.

The good news is that even now you can come to a place of deeper peace and greater freedom. It is my heartfelt hope that the short chapters in this book will help that happen for you. Each chapter has a message of its own, and you might find it helpful to pause after each chapter to reflect on what it has for you.

A disclaimer: I am not a scholar, a systematic theologian, or a licensed counselor. I have just enough education to know that I don't know much. Actually, I'm rather proud of my new self-description born of the pandemic: *I am a carrier of intelligence, but, I am often asymptomatic.* Mostly, I am a pastor who loves his people, a generalist who has studied a bit of all of this along the way.

More importantly, I struggle too. That's probably my strongest credential. As you will read, I come by my struggles honestly. I am excited to share with you some of the insights, stories, encouragements, and perspectives that have helped me come to a place of greater peace, freedom, and joy—a place of "enoughness."

You are worthy of that peace. You deserve to know that you are safe, you are loved, your life matters, and you are good enough just as you are. Because these things are true.

1

The Lesson of the Broken Crayon

There is no perfection,
only beautiful versions of brokenness.

SHANNON L. ALDER

Once I was visiting a buddy of mine while his daughter sat at the table coloring. She announced that she wanted to color something for me. As she earnestly set about her task, she pushed a bit too hard on one of her crayons and it broke. I wondered how she would respond. She paused for a second, then looked up to assure me: "It's OK. Broken things are good, too." With that, she took the broken part of the crayon still in her hand and continued to happily create a picture for me.

She was right. Broken things are good, too.

We are *all* broken on some level. We are all weak, all wounded. And unfortunately, most of us have not fully absorbed this deep-down truth: *It is OK to not be OK. It is OK to be broken.* Broken things *are* good.

Though it might be frightening at first to admit to ourselves that we are wounded and broken on some levels, it is ultimately freeing to do so. Our wounds can come from many sources:

from parents who pushed us too hard to fractured relationships to losses of all kinds.*

Later, I'll look in particular at the core wounds of childhood and how our coping mechanisms (which we needed for our own emotional survival) later get in the way. Perfectionism (and its sidekick, being a people-pleaser) are just such unconscious survival mechanisms. Though they helped us cope as kids, they now invariably distance us from greater joy and freedom. Yet, they are so ingrained in us that we often don't know how else to be.

And if you struggle with perfectionism, try too hard, or worry too much? It's OK. In no way does this diminish you or your goodness. For God, you are no less important and no less lovable. Each of us, whatever our struggles, no matter how badly we've messed up or how badly we've been treated, is worthy of love. Each of us matters greatly to this world.

One of my many heroes is the Jesuit priest Fr. Gregory Boyle. The work he does with gang members in the streets of Los Angeles is inspiring. He helps those gang members—most of whom were neglected, mistreated, or abandoned by parents—to find healing in a safe place. He helps them to know their dignity and to find hope as the beloved children of God that they are.

---

*Other possible sources of pain include such things as bodily wounds and physical challenges; job losses; parents who weren't there when we needed them or who were incapable of giving us what we most deeply needed; sexual or verbal abuse; eating disorders; fears that others would not accept our sexuality (maybe we're not sure we accept it ourselves); a failed marriage—and the hopes that died along with it; estranged relationships with children; business ventures that fell apart; past mistreatments; or perhaps patterns of addiction, sin, or shame.

4

Once I heard Fr. Boyle tell a story from his book *The Whole Language*. He described a visit to Pelican Bay State Prison, which houses inmates deemed hardened and the most violent. The prison organized a performance by the wonderfully talented pianist Eric Genuis, who brought along a small string section. His plan was to play for forty-five minutes, then allow time for questions.

Eric began to play, and the music touched everyone gathered. They were all deeply moved, held in silence. Soon, the prisoners were all sobbing and the guards were discreetly wiping away their own tears. When he finished, Eric turned and asked if there were any questions. There was only silence. Eventually, one gang member, his face fully covered with tattoos, rose. He had something to say but was still crying, so it was difficult for him. He could finally utter his one-word question: "Why?" When Eric heard the question, he realized what the inmate was asking and began to cry as well. "Because you are deserving," Eric replied. "You are worthy of beauty and music. And because there is no difference between you and me."

Whatever your struggles, God knows that *you* are worthy. Yes, we are each broken, and always will be. Yet, no matter our mistakes or where life has taken us in the past, underneath what people see on the outside—below all that we feel and think—is no less than a child of God: intact and good; wanted and loved; unique and important; seen and safe; and deeply united with the God who created us and whose love will never end.

Or, as that wise young girl with the broken crayon put it, "Broken things are good, too."

2

What Do You Think God Is Like?

Once you know the God of love,
fire all the other gods.

MIRABAI STARR

Shortly after I was ordained a priest, a woman told me that she greatly loved each of her children, of course, but, that she had an extra tenderness for the youngest who was born with no hand on his left arm. She described to me what it was like when the day that she feared finally happened. Her little boy came home from kindergarten that afternoon trying unsuccessfully not to cry. He explained that one of his classmates asked him what happened to his arm. He told everyone listening that he was born that way. Most of the kids seemed fine with that answer, but one of his classmates said, "That's weird," and several others laughed. The little boy didn't know a person could ever feel that lonely.

Mom comforted him a while, then looked him right in the eyes and said slowly and carefully, "Please, Michael, you've got to know this. That boy just doesn't yet know what I know and what God knows; that you are one of the most amazing people

6

God ever made. I love you just as you are—so much so that I couldn't possibly love you any more than I already do. So does God. Michael, God thinks you are wonderful, just as you are. God always will." The little boy buried his face in mom's arms and cried.

In his mom's love in that moment, the young boy experienced no less than the love of God. For God shows up for us most often in the goodness of the ordinary people of our regular lives. The love in that mom's heart for her little boy is exactly the kind of love God has for each of us.

A vital question for us to reflect on: What do we think God is like? More than one spiritual leader has said that—more important than believing that there *is* a God—is what we believe God is *like*. That's how crucial that question is.

So, what *do* you think God is like? Sadly, we sometimes stop wrestling with that question early in life. Maybe we settle on something we heard growing up. You know, Dad or Mom said something about God when we were a kid, or a teacher or priest gave us some image of God, and we assume all our lives that this is what God must be like. We filter all our life's experience through this often distorted and usually extremely limited way of thinking.

In truth, everything we could possibly say to describe God's goodness ultimately falls tremendously short of the reality of the wonders of God. Father Michael Himes, a theologian at Boston College, put it this way, "The least wrong thing we can say about God is that God is love."

If I had to pick only one word to describe God (and happily I don't) the word I'd choose would be "goodness." The goodness in that mom's heart for her child is the same goodness in

God's heart. It's the same goodness I've been blessed to see in people at every age of my life's journey. When I'm at my best, I am blessed to experience this goodness in my own heart too.

Most likely, if you struggle with perfectionism, you are pretty good at beating yourself up. You don't need anyone else to tell you you're not good enough, that you don't measure up, that no one, no God, would deem you worthy of being truly loved just as you are. You do that to yourself.

How deeply God must wish you knew differently. God is *delighted* to claim you as God's child. God wants you to know you are loved and treasured as you are and more than you could ever know.

When that sad little kindergartner heard his mom say "I love you just as you are—so much so that I couldn't possibly love you any more than I already do," in his loneliness he heard the very voice of God. For that was God's love in his mom's heart for the little boy. It's the love at the heart of the universe. It is the love in God's heart for you this moment—and in every moment of every day.

3

Is Your Brain Your Friend?

You can get the monkey off your back,
but the circus never leaves town. ·

ANNE LAMOTT

It might be a comfort to know there are genetic and biological components to perfectionism. From an evolutionary standpoint, our brains have a "negativity bias," meaning we're more likely to think about what might go wrong than what might go right. This makes sense. The chances of survival for our ancient ancestors increased if they were cautiously aware that there might be a saber-toothed tiger lurking behind the bushes. That is also why we are more likely to remember negative experiences than positive ones.

In our struggles with perfectionism, our fears are less of physical harm and more of emotional harm. But to the part of our brain that gets activated, it still feels like our very survival is at stake. Fearing we might be criticized, embarrassed, or rejected can feel as dangerous to us as the sight of a hungry animal intent on having us for dinner.

Our brain is wrong about this. It is good to be gentle with ourselves about such fears. Yet, we don't want to give our exaggerated fears more power than they deserve. A deep-down part of us is afraid that if other people knew our imperfections or inadequacies, they would reject us. Perhaps subconsciously, we believe that if people saw our flaws or failures, we would be left alone, unloved, and unsafe in a dangerous world. So, without realizing we are doing it, to avoid rejection, we set impossibly high expectations for ourselves. Deep inside, we may believe that others are already holding us to those same standards. When we inevitably fail to meet our learned expectations, our anxiety and discouragement only increase.

So, is your brain your friend? As with all important things, the answer is yes and no.

Comedian Emo Philips made me laugh when he put it this way: "I used to think my brain was the most vital part of my body," he said. "Then I realized that it was my brain telling me this." The truth hidden in his humor is that it is important to be able to assess our thoughts with detached objectivity. It's important to be aware of the effects of some of our reflexive thinking patterns.

We do ourselves a great service when we identify, without judgment, the thoughts about ourselves and the world that are inaccurate and harmful—but not let them dominate. Instead, we can work to embrace healthier, more loving ways of seeing the world and our place in it.

Certainly, all our anxieties and fears will not go away simply by changing our thoughts. Much of this is so deeply ingrained in us that it has become a reflex response to our world. We cannot think our way out of all our fears. Still, it makes a profound difference if we can learn healthier, more accurate, more loving ways to view ourselves and who we are in the world.

Some would say that going from our head to our heart is one of the longest, most challenging journeys we face. But a successful voyage is possible for each of us if we take advantage of help along the way.

Most find it helpful to have a trusted person to whom we can safely express our fears and struggles. It is important, if we can, to create a safe distance from those who try to shame us, from those who can't see our goodness. On the journey from head to heart, self-compassion and tending to our physical needs can be a healing balm for our souls. There are spiritual practices that can open us up to all that is loving, good, and true in ourselves and the universe.

Of course, the brain is not our enemy. But at times we need to remind our brain that there is no saber-toothed tiger lurking around the corner. We are safe right now. And in each moment, we do well to remind ourselves that we already have inside ourselves what we need to be OK, that we are resilient and resourceful, important and good, seen and loved, just as we are.

4

Shame Is NOT Your Friend

I wish I could show you the astonishing light of your own being.

HAFIZ

When our grade school's beloved art teacher retired after many years, we asked her to address the whole school community. As she spoke briefly, she said one sentence I will never forget: "Never apologize for your art."

When you were a kid, did you hear messages like that? I hope that, along the bumpy journey of childhood, when you colored outside the lines someone encouraged you. When it was needed, I hope you were forgiven, and as you grew, the best in you was lovingly nurtured.

How freeing to be taught that we did not need to apologize for our art. Sadly, many of us were made to feel instead that not only was our art not good enough but that *we* weren't good enough. Maybe we were even told with a look, or with words, "You should be ashamed of yourself!"

No. No, you should *not* be ashamed of yourself! For each of us there is an important place for healthy guilt. Guilt is my sorrow at the harm caused by the wrong I've done or by the good I didn't do. We need to say we are sorry and to make amends when we can.

But guilt is different from shame. Guilt is for the harm we've caused others, but shame focuses inwardly. Shame tells us that we are flawed as persons. Our weaknesses and sins lead us to conclude that we are deep-down defective and unworthy of love. Guilt and contrition are important and valuable, but shame crushes our spirits.

Attempts to shame people do *not* help them to see the errors of their ways and to change. Authentic change does not come from a sense of inadequacy but from an appreciation of who we truly are. Shame pushes people into hiding, fosters addictions, and diminishes growth. No, shame doesn't work. Shame leaves scars.

If you are someone who does not struggle with shame, you are blessed. Countless people *do* struggle with shame, though most don't talk about it publicly.

Most perfectionists are not that way in all aspects of their lives. But when we fall short of some goal, or don't measure up to some standard we think others set for us, the unspoken internal belief is that we ourselves are inferior and unworthy of belonging. We feel shame.

In my experience as a priest of more than forty-three years, I see that shame is often carried around sexual sins, sexual abuse, or sexual struggles. In chapter 10, we'll look at the fear and shame many people also carry because of their bodies and what they look like. Unfortunately, there is also too much shame for the kinds of bodies we have.

Shame is often at the root of cutting, burning, eating disorders, addictions, and other self-destructive patterns. Sometimes we struggle to accept forgiveness for some sin or mistake of ours, believing we deserve to be shamed, and then shaming ourselves.

If you are being shamed in a relationship, in a church, or in an organization with power over you, please do what you can to protect yourself. Step away, even if you can do so only mentally. Find people who are safe and who accept you for who you are, as you are. You deserve to be seen, safe, and loved.

In addition to our shame about what we think is wrong with us, there is also the mistaken fear that God is ashamed of us. Please know: God is not ashamed of you. God will never shame you.

We know this is true because Jesus told us and showed us. He was always very tender with human failure, even human sin. One of the most striking things about Jesus is that he does not seem to be shocked or angered by human sin. In fact, he never appeared to be upset at sinners. Nor does he ever shame anyone. Instead, when Jesus saw people being shamed, he would jump to their defense. When he saw crowds, individuals, or religious leaders trying to shame someone, Jesus would put himself in harm's way to protect the person being shamed.

Whether or not it is easy for you to believe this, it is true: God is not ashamed of you. God does not want you to be shamed. Instead, here are two of the truest things about God that God wants each person to know:

1. You don't have enough power to make God stop loving you. You don't.

2. God never invites you to grow without first loving you just as you are. God loves you just as you are.

Although people might say, "You should be ashamed of yourself," God would say, "No. No, you shouldn't." Or, as the teacher at our school would say, "Never apologize for your art."

5

Laughter IS Your Friend

*Laughter is the closest thing
to the grace of God.*

KARL BARTH

A few years ago I heard a story about one of my heroes in our common struggle with perfectionism. It's about a grandmother getting up in years who lived alone. Because it was becoming too difficult to buy Christmas presents for each grandkid, she decided to send each one a card, include the words "Buy your own present," and enclose a check. As she drove away from the post office, she felt a sense of accomplishment about getting those cards mailed in plenty of time for Christmas—that is, until she returned home and found the stack of checks she had forgotten to enclose. That meant each grandchild opened an envelope from Grandma with nothing in it but a Christmas card inscribed with "Buy your own present."

When she realized what she had done, Grandma had the most wonderful response: She laughed and laughed and laughed at herself.

Over the next few days, she phoned each of the grandkids and had a laugh with them over it as well. She had come to know that mistakes are a part of everyone's life, including hers. Everyone loved her. How could they not? She had learned the wonderful skill of laughing at herself.

I want to be more like her. Wouldn't it be great to accept the fact that we all make mistakes and that it's OK when we do? It *is* OK. We *all* flub up and fall short. Like that grandmother, wouldn't it be good to just relax a bit and be able to laugh at our foibles?

Laughter is a gift for us all—especially if we struggle with perfectionism.

There is an ancient Russian Orthodox tradition at Easter to tell jokes because of the belief that Easter was the ultimate joke on death. Satan and the forces of evil thought they had won by killing Jesus. But God had the last laugh, raising Jesus to new life again. After his death, a group of his followers came to the tomb with broken hearts and saw that it was empty. They began to understand, and as they did so, they began to laugh. They laughed the profound laugh of deepest joy. Their laughter echoed down through the ages to us and gives us reason to laugh even now.

Our Scriptures open to us the reality that there is laughter in God's heart. "The one enthroned in heaven laughs," says Psalm 2:4. Love is ultimately triumphant. Life is stronger than death. Goodness wins. It could be argued that every time we laugh, we join in the laughter of God—the laughter that God put in the heart of the universe.

What makes you laugh? I hope some things do. The nineteenth-century philosopher, poet, and cultural critic George

Santayana put it this way: "The young man who has not wept is a savage, and the older man who will not laugh is a fool."

It has been shown that laughter is good for our bodies. I suggest that it is also good for the body of Christ.

In my hallway that I pass through many times each day, I have hung a picture of Jesus laughing, his head thrown back in a boisterous guffaw. It keeps my day in perspective, reminding me not to take myself too seriously. It reminds me that, in the big scheme of things, there is always more reason for joy than not.

You will never hear me deny the reality of the pain and heartache so tangible in today's world—and so often in your life, heart, and the lives of people right around you. The good and the bad don't cancel each other out. But love is ultimately victorious. There is indeed laughter in the very heart of God.

6

What Difference Do You Make?

No act of kindness, no matter how small, is ever wasted.

AESOP

It's time for a pop quiz. How many of these questions can you answer correctly?

1. Who were the last three Heisman Trophy winners for the most outstanding player in college football?
2. Name the four wealthiest people in the world in the year 1994.
3. Who were the Academy Award winners for best actor or best actress from 2010 to 2012?
4. What are the professions of the people with the five most-followed Instagram accounts in 2023?
5. Name the past three winners of the Pulitzer Prize.

How well did you do? Me? Had I not looked up the answers, I would not have known a single one. I'm pretty sure I'm not the only person like that. For a moment, these folks were at the top of their game, the best in their fields, the most popular at what they do. But eventually, the applause dwindles, the money goes to someone else, the awards are mostly forgotten.

Here's the second quiz. How many of *these* questions could you answer?

1. Name a teacher, religious leader, or mentor who taught you something important or who somehow made a difference in your life.
2. Describe someone you know personally whose goodness has inspired you.
3. Who was there for you during a difficult time?
4. Who believed in you or encouraged you?

It was easier to answer this second quiz, wasn't it? The people who make a difference in our lives are most commonly not the ones with the most awards, money, or fame. They are the ones who care. They are the ones whose goodness makes our world better.

Most of the people I know who struggle with perfectionistic tendencies also have this wonderful quality: a desire to make this a better world for others. For some, that yearning is a deep and profound ache in our hearts. I am one of those people.

Somehow, the way God made me, the way my parents raised me, and the way other influences have formed me over the years have left me with a deep yearning to make this world a better place in the time I have here. That all comes with a special compassion in my heart for the underdog, the poor, the picked-on, and the excluded.

This does not make me any better or any worse than anyone else. It's just how I was made.

It is painful for me to let go of the thought that I could have made a bigger difference for more people.

These days, several Scripture passages have come together to form this statement which helps me keep perspective on what my call is and what it is not: I plant some seeds. I water some seeds that others have planted. And I harvest some seeds that others have watered. It is my job to do the best I can and to live with integrity along the way. But the results do not depend on me.

My spiritual work these days has been trying to trust that this is enough.

You might be like me. You might be someone who sometimes also laments that you can't make more of a difference. If so, you might be comforted, as I was, by this story:

A woman who had taken her child to a concert by a great pianist was talking to her friend before the concert and didn't notice, until the lights were dimmed, that her son had slipped away. She anxiously looked for him, and—as the curtains opened and stage lights went up—saw to her horror that her son was sitting at the concert piano plunking out the tune "Twinkle, Twinkle, Little Star." At that very moment, the pianist came out to perform, saw the child and realized what was happening. So, he slipped in behind the young boy and whispered, "Keep playing." As the little boy played "Twinkle, Twinkle, Little Star" with one finger, the pianist placed his hands on either side and began to fill in a wonderful accompaniment—to the delight of the entire crowd.

So it is with our efforts. When we face the needs of the world and the sufferings of so many, we stand before great mystery. But we do not stand alone, without hope, or without something to offer. We do what we can, and then we do our best to let go. We choose to trust that God, the master musician, will fill in around us to make something wonderful from our simple efforts.

7

Imperfect Parenting

(The Only Kind There Is)

> *When my kids act up
> in public, I like to yell,
> "Wait until I tell your mother!"
> and pretend they're not mine.*
>
> ANONYMOUS

Someone once asked comedian Jim Gaffigan what it was like when his fifth child was born. "Imagine you're drowning," he replied. "And someone hands you a baby." From my observations, countless parents feel like that even with their first child.

Parenting is truly an adventure. I can't think of any adventure more exhausting and exciting, fulfilling and frustrating, terrifying and tremendous, heartbreaking and holy. Did I mention "impossible to do perfectly"?

In many years of priesthood, I have talked with numerous parents who are overwhelmed by it all, or who worry they are not parenting correctly. Of course, they're not. There is no such thing as perfect parenting.

Many parenting books leave people feeling more inadequate than before they read them. And most parents' social media posts include the cutest, most picture-perfect photos of their kids they can find. (In Appendix A I offer two brief reflections for children who wrestle with questions about self-worth.)

Sadly, many public speakers are painfully glib on the topic of parenthood. It hurts when I hear a priest or minister say something like "It's Mother's Day (or Father's Day), and we are all filled with great joy." No, we are not all filled with great joy.

Many people are grieving the death of a parent, grieving the relationship they never had with their parents, or grieving their own inability to have children. Plenty of parents are worried about their children, angry at them, or heartbroken because they are estranged from them. And some parents know the excruciating, inexpressible pain of having buried a child.

Parents, please know that your children are not a referendum on your parenting skills or a reflection of who *you* are. You are important and beloved whatever your children do or don't do, no matter how they are or aren't. You influence your children profoundly, but they are not you and you are not they. One of your most crucial jobs as a parent is to ensure that your children know you see them as they are and accept them for who they are. And you do this by loving them unconditionally in the ways that only you can.

There is no way to fully know in advance what will be needed. Things that seemed to work well for a child at a certain age no longer effective later. What works for one child may not work the same way for your next one.

Commenting on how parents change and adjust over the years, my friend Jerry told me of the time his oldest daughter said to her youngest brother, "I wish I had the parents you did." The adjustments and adventures don't end.

Some find that a sense of humor helps. When her children were young, my cousin Mickey said, "Many people set aside money for their children's education. Not me. I'm going to set aside money for counseling for them because I know I'm messing them up." She was only half joking.

If I were a parent, I'd find comfort in this statement from pediatrician Rebekah Diamond: "If you still think there's such a thing as perfect parenting just know that I'm a pediatrician and parenting author and my toddler is eating strawberries dipped in ketchup for dinner tonight."

The opportunities for letting go in parenthood are countless. They never end. Motherhood has been described beautifully as that incredible risk of having a part of your heart walk outside your body for the rest of your life.

For all dads and moms, one notion to let go is this: the thought that you could parent perfectly. Again, you can't. You do the best you can. Yes, there are important skills to learn and new approaches that will make a difference. For example, if you are a parent, you would do well to be aware of how you were disciplined so you can be intentional about how you discipline your own children. Typically, your first impulse may be to do the very things your parents did to you that you did not like and that did not help you. You can do things differently.

In any case, it does not all depend on you. Your desire to be a good parent is itself enough for God's grace to flow through you, even when you are not aware of it doing so. It strikes me that if you worry about being a good-enough parent, you probably are one.

I think that parents have a unique insight into God's heart. Parents of young ones sometimes tell me that, no matter their frustrations of the day, watching their child sleeping reminds them again of how much they love their son or daughter. If you are a mom or dad, I would argue that the love upwelling in your heart at moments like this is not only *what* God is like; it actually *is* God in you.

For all its lack of glory, for all the heartaches and struggles, yours is a beautiful and holy calling. Your love gives us a glimpse of the other-centered love at the heart of the universe, a glimpse into the other-centered love of God.

When days are really difficult—when tears gather in your eyes or even bring you sobbing to your knees—remember that you understand God in a way no one else can. And remember that God understands you as well. There is truly a special place in God's heart for you.

8

An Ordinary Day

*Wisdom is not something we have
to strive to acquire. Rather, it arises
naturally as we slow down and
notice what is already there.*

HAEMIN SUNIM

In the movie *The World According to Garp,* the title character
(played by Robin Williams) has the "Mr. Mom" role at home. At
one point, there is a montage of him living an ordinary day with
his kids: preparing breakfast; driving them to school while they
sing at the top of their lungs; going to the park after school;
doing normal, everyday activities. At the end of that montage,
we see him tucking the children into bed, giving them a kiss
on the brow, and quietly leaving the room. He is back in the
kitchen when his wife—the main breadwinner—comes home
from work. She asks how his day was, and he gives this most
amazing reply: "I had a wonderful life today," he says.

What would it take for you or me to be able to say that? Does
it even seem possible that we could experience a wonderful life
on any ordinary, imperfect day? I would argue that if you or I

27

could be *truly* present every day to all the normal, mundane activities—its rhythms of silence and interaction; of beauty and ordinariness; its setbacks and successes—then somehow, at the end of any regular day, you and I could also say, "I had a wonderful life today."

I will never deny the pain and suffering of life. Some days are just awful. But what about an ordinary day? So many people who have buried loved ones after an unexpected death tell me they would give anything just to have one ordinary, imperfect day with them again.

We often race so quickly through our days. We can be so anxious about what is ahead or distracted by so many things in the moment that we miss, or forget, the true blessings woven throughout.

Each day is a mixture of hope and heartache, fears and fun, blessings and brokenness, loss and laughter. For many, a day could only be considered wonderful if it included something extraordinary or dramatic—not just the ordinary, imperfect days of our lives. The reason is that we have fallen prey to the pernicious "If Only" syndrome.

The primary symptom is the presence of the words "if only" in our worldview. It starts at a young age. It appears in obvious ways in school-age kids when they think or feel things like: If only I had a phone, then I'd be happy. Or, if only I was in high school or college, then my real life would start. Or, if only I made that team. Or, if only she'd be willing to go out with me, then I'd have a reason to live. Or, if only I could get my own car, or enough likes on social media, then I would feel good about myself.

As we age, often it becomes: If only I was married, then I'd settle down. Or, if only we had our own kids, then we'd return to church and make a faith life.

On and on it goes. It's not long before the sentence becomes: "If only I could retire and get some time to breathe, then I'd live. Then, finally, the saddest "if only": "If only I could do it all over again. Then I'd really appreciate what I had while I had it." But then it's too late. We've let "if only" keep us from living the life we had while we had it. It's dreadful—and all too common.

The antidote? To be aware of the blessings woven into the ordinariness of life. Then to think again: What really brings me joy? Is it not around me—at least on some levels—right now?

As I will discuss in chapter 13, it's extremely challenging to find happiness inside ourselves. Yet, it is impossible to find it anywhere else. That is the great secret. Joy is available to us now, and each moment, for those of us awake enough to see it.

A question that has been important to me over many years of priesthood is "How does God show up in our lives? How does God come to us?"

The answer is found in this profound sentence from author and former psychotherapist Paula D'Arcy: "God comes to you disguised as your life." God comes to us in the ordinary, imperfect people around us; in the messes and the mixed-up times; in the loving and the letting go; in the laughter, fear, tedium, and heartache; and in what we find inside our own hearts. It's true: *God comes to us disguised as our lives.* There's no other way.

You and I are invited to be awake enough to more and more live this day—and each "this day"—so that at the end of it, should someone ask us, "How was your day?" our answer could be "I had a wonderful life today."

9

How Do You Compare?

(Hint: It's an awful question.)

*Be yourself; everyone else
is already taken.*

OSCAR WILDE

There is a world that is quite tempting, extremely addictive, and truly pervasive. It is also harmful and sometimes even deadly. It is the world of comparisons.

The world of comparisons takes our face in its hands, turning us away from the lives we have and from our own goodness to look at a world that doesn't exist—the lives we presume others have. Instead of seeing the blessings woven into our own daily lives, the world of comparisons tricks us into thinking that either we are better than others or we don't measure up.

Comparisons thrive in the seductive world of social media. It's obvious that most people post pictures of themselves looking their best and at the happiest of times. Usually, they seem to be enjoying themselves while doing something that they are good at or that they love.

Of course. Who posts a picture of their family having an argument or of themselves throwing up after drinking too much? When do we see people looking worriedly at their checkbook and the stacks of bills on their table? Who posts pictures of themselves baggy-eyed while slogging through piles of laundry with a crying child on their hip?

As we scroll through social media, most commonly our lives do not *feel like* what others' lives *look like* online. The insecurities and loneliness grab at our guts.

Of course, one does not have to have a social media account to get sucked into the world of comparisons. It used to be called "keeping up with the Joneses." It is sadly all too common even among children who compare their clothing, appearance, and, indeed, their very lives to others. The world of comparisons is all around us and, too often, in us.

When we compare ourselves to others, we find that there are always people more popular than we are; more attractive, more athletic, wealthier, more accomplished, smarter, with more likes and more followers. Comparing kills our souls. And the flat-out truth is: None of it matters at all!

Sometimes we compare ourselves to others as a way to feel superior. This also crushes life out of us. A study of the Gospels shows that Jesus never looked down on anyone, nor did he ever look up to anyone. Jesus always looked eye to eye at folks, and he invites us to do the same. We share a common humanity, are deep down more alike than different, and are no less precious and important because those things are true.

What is our way out of this hall of mirrors? Stepping away from the dangerous world of comparisons is crucial, difficult work. But it can be done—and there are many things that help.

One step is working to get our thinking right. As mentioned, in reality, nothing in the world of comparisons matters.

It doesn't! You are a precious child of God in real time. All the love in the universe is with you and in you each moment. Social media is not reality, but your precious life is. If you have trouble convincing yourself this is true, please find people you trust, those in whom you can confide, to help you see just how true it is.

If you can't talk to yourself effectively enough to go to a social media site without getting hooked by it, then don't go there. Take a sabbatical from social media. More and more, I hear from people who have found great freedom in doing just that. They wonder why they ever wasted so much time managing their image on their chosen platform, comparing what they see there instead of having a real life.

Most crucially, practice gratitude for your real life. We've got to practice being thankful. Though our brains are physically hardwired to hang onto negativity, fear, loss, and loneliness, they are not predisposed or taught to retain gratitude for our blessings. We have to intentionally train that part of the brain. There are many ways to nurture the joy and peace of a grateful heart. We'll talk about some of those in chapter 20.

The fact is, we can train ourselves to remember what is most true: that we are real; that we are loved; that we are good; that our lives matter; that we are profoundly blessed.

For everyone, living in the real world is sometimes really hard. But the world of comparisons is a dangerous place. The blessings right in front of me are so much more profound than anything I could ever see in that world. *I don't want to miss those blessings.* I pray for you, as well as for myself, that we don't miss the blessings of this one, ordinary, precious, imperfect, important life we've been given.

10

If Your Mirror Could Talk, What Would It Say?

Honestly, if I were two-faced,
would I be showing you this one?

ABRAHAM LINCOLN

Once, comedian David Letterman offered a Top Ten List titled "The Top Ten Things You Don't Want to Hear from a Talking Mirror." Here are two that made me laugh: "Sorry, this is what you look like" and "You're not really the mirror type."

They made me laugh because they were clever. They also made me sad because this reminded me that countless people live with a dreadful fear that this is exactly what we would hear if our mirrors could talk.

Healthy spirituality has been defined as, above all, seeing rightly. When it comes to looking at our bodies, what matters most is difficult to see.

A lot of our judgment about who we are comes from our sense of our bodies and what we see in the mirror. How many of us carry shame about our weight, regret about our age, fears about our health, or disappointments with how we look?

Women especially have been held up to airbrushed, unrealistic standards of "beauty" for so long.

Due to injuries, illness, genetics—or because we don't measure up to models we see in advertisements—most people will tell you there are plenty of things that they don't like about their bodies.

Of course, we are so much more than our bodies. But our bodies do matter profoundly. For the ancient Celts, the body was actually part of their scriptures. The body would remind them that God chose flesh to enter the world. Yet, God did not choose flesh just once in Jesus: God chose your flesh and mine in which to be embodied in this world.

We live in a culture of impossible physical ideals. A friend of mine who used to work on advertising photo shoots would tell me that *every* picture they ever used was photoshopped. Doesn't it become news sometimes when the paparazzi catch a photo of a star not wearing makeup? Even supermodels—genetically advantaged to begin with, perhaps cosmetically enhanced, and who enjoy the luxury of daily visits with a personal trainer—are careful about being seen without makeup. Well, gravity affects everyone, and they won't look like that forever, even with cosmetic surgery. Eventually, we all face the diminishments of age and the toll it takes on our bodies.

We can become slaves to unreal body images. More than just wasting our lives, we can cause ourselves real harm.

Once, on retreat, I took some time to apologize to my body. When I was playing sports in high school, I was taught to ignore pain and told that the hurt would go away if I played harder. That is also the approach I took through college sports and beyond. Though, for the most part, that approach seemed to work then, now I pay the price with distracting pains and often cantankerous joints. The human body does not forget. I wish I had learned when I was younger to listen more for the clear, simple wisdom it offered me.

As in most things, it can sometimes help to keep a sense of humor about it all. One of my favorite intentional misquotes is this redo of the talking mirror from *Snow White*: "Mirror, mirror, near the toilet, / I wake up hopeful and then you spoil it."

We hear rightly that mindfulness (being nonjudgmental and aware of one's thoughts and emotions) is a crucial skill to develop. We also need to develop a healthy "body-fulness." Fortunately, we can learn to appreciate the bodies we've been given and to be tender to them while we have them.

In Appendix B at the end of this book, "Our Bodies, Broken and Beloved," I offer a guided meditation that will invite you to bring your body to God, just as it is. If you sometimes think you don't measure up, the truth is that God loves you and the body you've been given.

One day, we will have to give up our imperfect bodies as we know them. For now, they hold who we are. As our Celtic ancestors taught us, our imperfect, sometimes wounded bodies also hold God.

11

Moments of Perfection in Our Imperfect Lives

(Three Stories)

*If you want others to be happy,
practice compassion.
If you want to be happy,
practice compassion.*

DALAI LAMA

As a young mom, despite feeling overwhelmed by all the demands of work and motherhood, Brie still tried to have an active prayer life. Once she carved out time to attend a workshop on contemplative prayer.

To the other participants Brie described herself as being a frustrated young mom who is pulled in too many directions all the time to try a contemplative prayer approach. It all seemed like too much in the midst of juggling life and work and fussy babies.

At one point at the workshop she spoke up and said, "Where is the icon of the contemplative mom with one baby on the hip and a crying kid on the floor and burning food on the stove and trying to do work on the laptop on the side and feeling like I get up early in the morning to try to pray and that it doesn't matter how early I get up, because my kids are always going to interrupt my morning prayer time anyway?"

The workshop leader responds: "OK, Brie, you be you and I'll be God." He proceeds to speak on behalf of God in front of the class. "Brie, it means so much to me that you get up early to try to pray. I see how much you love me and that you even get up early to spend this time with me, and I can't tell you how much it means." He ends by saying: "You see, Brie, you're so precious to me and I just love you so much, I can't bear it. So, what I do, Brie, is rush into the bodies of your children and wake them up because I want to know what it feels like to be held by you."

Brie started sobbing and every person in the room was wiping tears from their eyes. For Brie, in the midst of the impossible demands of being a young mom, God wanted to know what it felt like to be held by her. So, God rushed into the bodies of her children to wake them. God came to Brie.

That is just what our God does. In the blessed mess of this world and these times in which we live, God comes. God loves us so much that God rushes to be with us.

* * * * *

Ted was a retired schoolteacher. Several years ago, I led the funeral services for Ted's younger brother, Artie, who died at age sixty-one. Artie had Down syndrome and lived at home with Ted. Ted was a kind and gentle man who spent his life taking care of Artie, and his aged mom until she died.

Some would think that Ted did not have much of a life. He certainly let go of a lot to care for his mom and for his brother. But if you knew Ted you saw that he got it. He had deep wisdom and a sense of quiet peace.

When I saw Ted a few weeks after the funeral, I asked him what it was like to be him after burying Artie. He moved me deeply with his answer. He said: "I am so grateful, Father Joe. You see, Artie needed me; there was no one else to care for him." Then he started crying and said, "For years, my prayer has been that I would live at least one day longer than Artie so I could take care of him. My tears are because I am just so grateful that I did."

I hope you've met people like Ted. People whose humble goodness has encouraged you. People whose goodness gives us a glimpse of the goodness of the heart of God.

Not only do I hope you've met people along the way like that, I also hope you've had people who have loved you that way. For God loves you with that kind of humble, faithful, self-sacrificing love.

* * * * *

Paysach Krohn tells heartwarming stories of human goodness. In his book *Echoes of the Maggid*, he tells of a memorable speech that speaks beautifully of the question of perfection in the reality of our imperfect daily lives.

A dad was speaking at a fundraiser for a Jewish school that serves learning disabled children. After thanking the dedicated staff he tells them that he'd always been taught that everything God does is filled with perfection. He plaintively asks where

God's perfection is to be found in his son who can't read or add or understand the same way as other kids.

He then answers his own question. He tells them that God's perfection is to be found in the way people react to such children.

He describes the day he and his son Shaya walked past a park where some boys that Shaya knew were playing baseball. Shaya wondered if they'd ever let him play. The father knew his son was not at all athletic and doubted they would but was given the OK by one of the players.

In the ninth inning and with his team losing, it was now Shaya's turn to bat. When the pitcher noticed Shaya didn't even know how to properly hold the bat he moved a few steps closer and lobbed the ball softly to try to help Shaya hit it. One of Shaya's teammates came up to help him hold the bat, and together they swung and hit a soft ground ball to the pitcher.

The pitcher picked it up and purposely threw it into right field, far beyond reach of the first baseman. Everyone told Shaya to keep running and he did so as the opposing players intentionally kept throwing the ball wide of the mark. With the kids cheering him on, Shaya ran all the way until he tagged home plate. His teammates lifted him on their shoulders and made him the hero. Shaya had just hit a "grand slam," winning the game for his team!

Through his tears, the father told those gathered that—on that day—those eighteen boys reached their level of God's perfection. They did.

Sometimes we forget: Life is hard. Life is beautiful. And we are ultimately all on the same team.

If you're ever the one who feels you don't quite fit in, the one on the outside looking in, I hope there are people there for you like those kids were for Shaya that day—people who listened to the impulse to be the kind, compassionate human beings they truly were. For you also deserve that love.

And if you notice someone on the fringes who doesn't seem to quite fit in, someone who is awkward or in pain, I hope that you will listen to that same impulse stir in you to be the loving and compassionate person you already truly are. For in moments like that, when you and I act with compassion and inclusion, we reach our level of God's perfection in our lives.

12

The Goal

*My goal was to lose ten pounds
this year. Only fifteen to go.*

TITLE OF A DIETING NOTEBOOK

There is a purpose for setting goals. There is value to having
them. Goals can help us name, and remember, what is important to us. They can help us be intentional about living as we
move through our days. Unfortunately, goals can also lead us
to miss the life we have while we have it.

If you are someone with perfectionistic tendencies, trying
to completely rid yourself of perfectionism is not a good goal.
Your perfectionistic energy is part of the true gift you bring to
the world. It is one ingredient in the complex recipe that makes
you *you*. And no one can do a better job of being you than you!

The goal is not to rid ourselves of being perfectionistic.
(Some even become perfectionists about not being perfectionistic!) The goal is to become more at peace with who we are and
to live our days with joy and meaning. Our perfectionist energy
can help us do just that.

When it is healthy, perfectionist energy can be used for great good to help us thrive. It can help us see how this world could be and motivate us to do our part to make that happen. But when perfectionist energy is unhealthy, it can cause harm, even great harm. It is important to learn to draw upon the best of perfectionistic energy while stepping away from its destructive power. There are ways to think and perspectives to keep that can help us do just that.

Here is one: If you've ever been in a car with children for a long drive, there's a good chance you have heard the question "Are we there yet?" The tone usually implies, "Why *aren't* we there yet?"

As you and I make our way along the journey of life, we often have the same question. We think that when we arrive *there*, life will finally be good. We are frustrated that we are not yet there. The desired destination may be that we have finally attained the weight we wanted, the salary we deserve, the number of social media "likes" we hoped for, or any of the innumerable things indicating "We have arrived!"

It doesn't work. Life doesn't start when we get to some destination. The journey itself is what matters most. This day is what we have. This day, with its disappointments and delights, its trials and tenderness, its loss and laughter—this is it! Learning to be present in the moment, to the journey itself, yields blessings beyond measure.

Once I talked with a young man who was training for the Olympics. He worked to keep this kind of perspective. He was a phenomenal athlete. Not only was he naturally gifted; he also worked his tail off. He described to me his punishing training schedule, and I asked what it was like to be him in the midst of it all.

He said that he would sometimes get jealous of his friends. Unlike them, he'd often start his day at 3:30 AM. He couldn't eat what his friends ate or do some of the fun things they did. He missed many family vacations and spent countless hours in grueling, often lonely training.

When I asked him how he coped with the challenges, setbacks, and daily grind, he said, "Everyone says, 'Keep your eyes on the finish line.'" Then he countered, "But I'm telling you, it can't be just that. It can't just be keeping your eye on the finish line. I know how many athletes never get there—the hundreds of thousands like me who have trained like I trained, worked like I worked, whose parents sacrificed like mine did, but who never get there. Their time wasn't quite good enough, or they blew a knee or a shoulder."

"You have to find something along the way," he said. "You have to know that you are a person, not just an athlete. The victory lane and the finish line don't come for us all. You have to learn that your life matters *now*."

Such great wisdom in such a young person. In the end, this young man never competed in the Olympics. He came close, but he didn't qualify. He was both greatly disappointed and simultaneously just fine. He is OK because he knew the truth. It was never just about the finish line. It was always about the journey itself.

For some of us, the hope of the finish line, the dream of what could be, might help us keep going. For each of us, the true goal is found only in the journey itself.

13

The Path: Living Inside Out

When things change inside you, things change around you.

UNKNOWN

If you are familiar with the classic story *The Wizard of Oz*, you know that the main characters are a scarecrow, a lion, a tin man, and a girl named Dorothy who set out on an adventure to find what they believe they deeply need. They each hope the wizard can give them the thing they are missing that would make them whole. The four become friends on their amazing journey and help one another out along the way. In the end, they each find that they already had what they needed inside themselves all along.

This is also our story. As we make our way together on our journey, we often feel we are inadequate, that there is something missing in us. Whatever it is we need, we know it's somewhere "out there," and we desperately think we've got to find it. In the end, we can find it only where it has been all along. It is already in us.

Me? I spent too much of my life trying to prove to the world that I was good enough, hoping that I could then believe it myself. I thought that if I could just live in such a way that everyone else thought I was good enough, then I could finally accept that I was too.

Like most people who struggle with perfectionism, I long made the mistake of wondering, "Am I good enough for everyone else?" The truth is, there is no way I will ever be good enough for everybody—that I will ever be everything that everyone wishes. I needed to grieve that this old way of thinking does not work. While we all need outside encouragement and support, I began to take in the sobering reality that no one else could ultimately give me what I needed to find in myself. My sense of self-worth that I hoped to find in others? I had to learn to find it in myself. The question I needed to ask is not if I am good enough for others. The question is "Am I good enough for me?"

How about you? Are you good enough for you? Here's a different way to say this: We are called to live from the inside out. Our temptation is to live in the other direction. The wounded parts of ourselves think we need to do all kinds of things to earn love. The frightened places in us think we need to make ourselves as successful and error-free as possible to be acceptable. Some unspoken and unexamined drive in us keeps telling us that we need to be more attractive, pure, pious, and countless other things to be worthy of believing in.

You don't need any of that. You are already good. You are loved and lovable as you are. You are important and valuable for who you are. What you need is already in you.

"It is difficult to find happiness within oneself, but it is impossible to find it anywhere else," said German philosopher Arthur Schopenhauer. More and more, I hope you can exhale and be at peace with yourself as you are: that you can spend less time trying to prove your worth and more time just enjoying being you. Now. Not when, not if. Now, as you are.

As we follow the journey of those four characters on the yellow brick road to meet the wizard of Oz, we begin to realize that the lion was already a mixture of fear and bravery, and always would be. The scarecrow often doubted he had a brain, yet his thoughts consistently led the crew in the right direction. The tin man who thought he needed a heart was already tender and compassionate. Dorothy helped create a sense of home for her friends even on the way to the home she deeply longed for.

The joy and peace you long for is not to be found somewhere over the rainbow. It's in you now.

14

The Wounds of Childhood

*I just wish everyone could know
that they are enough.*

HEATHER SOUSAN, STYLIST,

WHILE CUTTING MY HAIR

It's not surprising that I struggle with perfectionism. Though I was too young to name it as such, perfectionism was how I tried as a child—without realizing it—to cope with the wounds I received growing up.

My dad was a good man who worked hard, trying to help raise six children in a small house without much money. At age sixty-seven, Dad was out buying a Christmas tree with Mom when he had a brain aneurysm. As we gathered around his bed that night, there was a moment when no one else was in the room. Though Dad would never regain consciousness, I chose that opportunity to thank him, to tell him I loved him, and to tell him I forgave him. I forgave him for "the Look."

The Look was the expression of disdain Dad shot my way sometimes when, in his estimation, I fell short. It felt to me as if he was trying to tell me, *I am disgusted with you as a person.*

For many, the Look might not have seemed like much. Yet, it mattered greatly to me. It mattered so much to me especially because of something my mom would do.

Mom had a good heart and a tough life. It was less the poverty of her childhood that scarred her and more likely the abuse she suffered. When Mom would get mad, she would yell, go to her room, slamming the door behind her, and then give us the silent treatment. I hated that. I felt frightened by this abandonment. It truly felt that love had gone away. It seemed that love went away too often.

Six-year-old me internalized those two things from my parents this way: *If I am not good enough, love will go away.* So, I became the pleaser, the one who tried to earn love and do everything as perfectly as possible to avoid whatever might make love disappear again. The tension felt like a pit in my stomach. I still feel that pit sometimes even now. You may carry wounds from childhood, too.

Perfectionism is, in part, one of the ways a child might try to cope with the challenges they knew growing up. It is actually for our own emotional survival that we take on coping roles such as perfectionism. Some of us become people-pleasers. Others become the hard-charging person that no one will mess with. Many become the rule-follower, often looking for some structure outside ourselves that we can devote ourselves to for our security because we don't trust that we have inside ourselves what we need to be OK.

There are other roles we might adopt. On one level, these can be strengths and a gift to the world. But it is also important to know this: No matter which coping mechanisms arose in us as children, they will never give us the sense of peace, safety, and joy for which we yearn. Perfectionism, like all other coping mechanisms, just won't do it. Although we needed them as a means of emotional survival when we were young, as we get older, they inevitably, universally, get in the way.

The wonderful news is that we can truly become freer. We can find ways to live that are filled with joy and peace. At the same time, we never completely outgrow the tendency to fall back on old ways of coping. They will appear in us especially at times of transition, tension, or fear.

Given my tendency to feel that if I'm not perfect (or close to it) then love will go away, you might understand why one Sunday, I found myself peeking at the pews through a crack in the church sacristy door. It was shortly after I became a pastor, and taking on that role for the first time was quite frightening. So much was new, and the challenges felt daunting. With the heartache of saying goodbye to my previous parish still fresh, I was now living in a new place with new people, in a new job, with new and bigger responsibilities. It was all so overwhelming.

That first weekend, I introduced myself at each Mass, and tried so hard to give the best homily I possibly could. It's sad for me to remember this now, but the following weekend I found myself peeping through the little crack between the church sacristy wall and door, a scared child inside, wondering if anyone would come back. Though I rationally knew better, some part of me still felt like it all depended on me and that if I didn't do a good enough job, love would go away.

I'm happy to report the folks did come back, and I was blessed to serve that vibrant parish for almost sixteen years. Yes, I still sometimes try too hard and worry too much. But now, twenty-five years later, I am freer and more alive. I savor the deeper peace that I know in my daily living. And I greatly want you to experience that peace, too, so you can know what I have come to know: Our growing-up wounds can have less and less power over us. We can become more alive and free! It takes work to experience this inner freedom and deeper peace. But the results of those efforts are a gift beyond measure.

15

The Most Important Word?

You are imperfect, permanently and inevitably flawed. And you are beautiful.

AMY BLOOM

When I work with people after the death of a loved one, I speak with them about one of the most important truths I know: The good and bad, the happy and sad of life, don't cancel each other out.

I am grateful that I believe there is a life beyond this one, a life beyond what I can see. That belief, however, does not remove the sorrow I feel when people I love get sick and die. Yet, in the midst of all the heartache and letting go, kindnesses will appear in surprising ways. Those kindnesses don't eliminate the painful feelings of sorting through a loved one's possessions or facing that first holiday, anniversary, or birthday without them. But none of that pain diminishes the great promise that love is forever.

When a loved one dies, of course it is OK to cry. We would not hurt so much if we did not care. It's also OK to laugh. We do not dishonor the memory of a loved one if we sometimes have joy.

Recently, I presided at the funeral service for a young man, Paul, who died after a brief fight with two aggressive cancers. Paul was a great guy, and I loved working with him. His wife, Mary Grace, was known for her sense of humor and made me laugh several times through my tears. One of those times was during the beautiful and moving eulogy she gave at the start of the service.

After Mary Grace gratefully acknowledged the large turnout, she added: "As you know, Paul was very competitive. Well, I am, too," she said. "I see how many people there are here today, and I want you to know that I expect at least one more person than this at my funeral."

Now I was again crying *and* laughing. There is the crucial word: *and*. The word *and* is one of the most important words in any language. For many, there is comfort in *either/or* thinking. Something is either this or it is that. But the more we authentically develop our spiritual lives, the more we realize that reality is *both/and*, not either/or.

In a Gospel passage from Matthew, Jesus puts it this way: Let the weeds and the wheat grow together. We would prefer having the pleasant and good things in life—the wheat—only. We might think we could, and should, pull the weeds from this world, from a situation, or from ourselves. But we can't. Trying to do so leads to all sorts of violence. Yes, we work to become more loving and Christlike human beings and to help build a more just and loving world. But both weeds and wheat will always be there. All of life, and each of us, is always a mixture of both. So, Jesus tells us: Let the weeds and wheat grow together.

Can we come to peace with accepting that we ourselves are a mixture of both? Can we accept that weeds grow in us and among everyone—along with the wheat?

Like me, you may initially be discouraged by the thought that, in life, there will always be weeds among the wheat. Jesus, however, knows that this awareness helps us be fully alive and free. Because this is truth. It is one of the most profound and important truths of all: Life is both/and, not either/or.

Given all this discussion of wheat and weeds, perfection and imperfection, some might question this quote from Jesus: "So be perfect, just as your heavenly Father is perfect" (Matthew 5:48). In using the word *perfect*, Jesus is telling us to be whole, complete; to live with integrity and inclusion. Some Scripture scholars suggest that the location of this passage in Jesus' teaching means he is focusing on being fully compassionate and merciful. Indeed, Luke's version of this same Gospel verse translates as "Be merciful, just as [also] your Father is merciful" (6:36). Jesus wants us to grow in our capacity for love and mercy, including being loving and merciful toward ourselves— not to strive for flawlessness.

In the spiritual realm, we often grow much more by getting stuff wrong than by doing it right. The only perfection available to us is the honest and gentle acceptance of our own imperfection.

Our friends in twelve-step programs typically understand this much better than most of us. At Alcoholics Anonymous meetings, folks don't say, "I *used to be* an alcoholic." They say, "I *am* one." This is great wisdom.

"I've been clean and sober for twelve years," one of my friends said. "But naming out loud that I am still an alcoholic reminds me that I need a support system around me, that I've got to keep doing my work. If I act like that is not in me, I'll try to fool myself that I can go back to my old ways and be fine." We all need to know that we will always carry our wounds and our weaknesses. Again, awareness is everything.

We are each such a mixture of wheat and weeds:

- We are at once sinners and, at the same time, loved by God—loved with an intensity beyond imagining.
- In a world that is frightening and fragile, we are at the same time profoundly safe in the heart of God.
- We are as grains of wheat in the vast field of the earth yet, at the same time, each remarkably precious and unbelievably beloved.

Yes, the good and the bad, the happy and the sad of everything—and everyone—don't cancel each other out. They don't in this world, nor in you or me.

Life is both/and. It's one of the truest things I know.

16

Are You a Worrier?

There were many terrible things in my life, and most of them never happened.

AUTHOR UNKNOWN

In Thornton Wilder's play *Our Town*, a young woman named Emily Gibbs dies. She pleads to return to Earth for just one day. Emily is told that she wouldn't like it because she'd have to live it just like she did, and no one but her would know she was back for just one day. She pleads and argues, and they finally let her go.

Emily chooses to go back on her twelfth birthday: she observes the world from her precious vantage point of having only one day to see it again. She is heartbroken to discover that no one seems to savor this one precious day with her while they have it. One of the things that strikes her is the worried looks on people's faces. "I never realized before how troubled... live persons are," she says. "From morning to night, that's all they are—troubled."

So are we. We are troubled, frightened. We worry. When we wonder if we will get good grades, or whether our children will thrive, we are troubled. When our car makes a noise we haven't heard before or our body gets a lump we haven't felt before, we are frightened. When a conversation doesn't go well and we don't know what to say or do next, we worry. We are worried, troubled, and frightened by so many things. Perfectionists tend to carry anxiety and fear more than most. We are, of course, not the only ones who do so.

From God we get a different and consistent message: "Do not be afraid." We are offered peace instead of fear.

When Jesus invites us to follow him on the way, he never promises that life will be easy or that faith will take away our burdens or free us from our sufferings and losses. Instead, he seems to go out of his way to make sure we know the journey will be difficult.

Jesus senses his own cross of suffering and death looming on the horizon even as he invites us to be unafraid. He tells us not to worry because just as he trusted that God would be with him, even through "the valley of the shadow of death" (Psalm 23:4), God will be with us as well. And Jesus tells us not to worry because he knows that worry robs us of life.

Worry has a corrosive power that eats away at our bodies, relationships, and peace of heart and mind. Worry does not help in any way. If you are a worrier, ask yourself: Do you think bad things didn't happen because you worried about them? Worry doesn't change the outcome of future things. It does not prevent loss or heartache. Instead, worry keeps us from the blessings of our days as we have them. Worry robs us of the life and joy that are found only in the present.

There is a different way. When we notice we are getting frightened or nervous, it is good to name what we are feeling, to gently acknowledge our worry and fear. If we can, we remind ourselves that we are safe in that very moment and choose to trust that God is with us right then.

The next step? Jesus offers this: After Jesus offered his followers peace and told them to be unafraid, he would then invite them to follow his way, to choose love. Our next step is the same. We choose again to love. We become aware that we are alive in that very moment and again choose kindness, goodness. We acknowledge our anxiety, but we don't stay there.

Yes, we sometimes plan for the future. We have to think ahead and use our brains. We just don't live in the future. Nor should we act like the past didn't happen and not learn from it. We just don't live there either. Whatever our worries, tensions, regrets, or fears, we only have to love now. That's all we really can do. That's all we need to do. It is the path to a holy, happy, joy-filled life.

Though Emily Gibbs had been excited about the thought of going back to earth for her twelfth birthday, the experience itself was painful. It made her sad to watch so many troubled, worried people race through their day. During her brief moments with her mom and dad before they hustle off to the burdens of the day, she desperately wishes they would savor this one day they had together. "I love you all, everything," Emily cries inside. "I can't look at everything hard enough. Oh, Mama, just look at me one minute as though you really saw me."

But no one else could see the shortness of life as she could, and it breaks her heart. When it comes time to go back, she asks for one more look and says sadly, "Goodbye...Mama and Papa. Goodbye to clocks ticking. And Mama's sunflowers. And food and coffee....And sleeping and waking up!" And she ends with these poignant words: "Oh earth, you are too wonderful for anyone to realize you."

Jesus offers a different way. Instead of worries that keep us from being truly alive in the time we have on earth, he offers us peace. He invites us not to worry. He invites us to love now.

17

Everything Worth Doing Is...

*Whatever you do, always give
one hundred percent.
Unless you're donating blood.*

BILL MURRAY

Some who read this chapter's title will likely make it a full sentence in their minds without even realizing it. "Everything worth doing is worth doing well" goes the old saying. If you believe this, then I would say to you, "No, it isn't." Seriously.

The first time I remember hearing this saying differently was when I was in my early thirties. At a stressful time in my life, someone I trusted said to me, "Not *everything* worth doing is worth doing well." It took me quite a while to absorb that, but he was right.

Studies suggest that almost everyone has some areas in their lives where perfectionistic tendencies are at play. And most perfectionists are not that way in every aspect of their lives. But for many of us, we strive way too hard in way too many areas.

Maybe you are like me in this regard. Since childhood, some part of me tried to prove to the world that I was good enough to be wanted and loved. Therefore, some things that didn't matter much became more important than they really were. They became a preconscious referendum on my own worth and goodness. Trying so hard all the time often yielded an unrelenting tension that was both understandable and sad.

No, everything worth doing is not worth doing well. As I described in chapter 13, the path to healing and peace involves learning to increasingly live inside out. We can then discover ways to come to peace with who we are as individuals. Our goodness is not defined by how we perform in any given moment or by what others think of our performances. Nor is it defined by how our yard looks, how our children are dressed, or whether we are in jail. Nor is our goodness defined by a grade we got in a course or whether a relationship lasted. Our goodness isn't defined by any of the countless expectations we impose as proof of our worthiness. Instead, our value comes from *who we are* as beloved children of a loving God.

We are loved as we are. Whatever we do or don't like about ourselves, whatever happens to us or doesn't, whatever others might think of us (or whether they think of us at all), our goodness is intrinsic. In our unique ways, we each love this world and do our parts to make it a bit better than how we found it. That's enough. That's all that matters.

A brilliant friend of mine told me about an adage that is often used by our brothers and sisters in twelve-step programs. It has had a great effect on me: "What other people think of me is none of my business." Now *that* is a sentence worth remembering and taking to heart, for it is profound wisdom. No, everything worth doing is *not* worth doing well. But what will others think of me? That is truly none of my business.

18

1968 and the Lesson of Apollo 8

There's truth that you can never know intellectually.

KIERRA C.T. BANKS

Many who read this book are probably not old enough to remember the events of 1968. In many ways, it was a year like this one. Although filled with many blessings and much goodness, 1968 was also a time of struggle. A long, difficult conflict raged out of control in Southeast Asia. It was the year of the Tet Offensive, which convinced many Americans that the Vietnam War was a hopeless cause.

On a quiet April evening in 1968, the leader of the civil rights movement would be gunned down as he stood on a balcony of the Lorraine Motel in Memphis. The assassination of Dr. Martin Luther King Jr. would lead to unrest and riots across America: Baltimore, Kansas City, Washington DC, and practically every major US city. Two months after that assassination, Bobby Kennedy, who was running for president of the United States, was also assassinated.

It was a year not unlike the present—full of upheaval, messiness, and chaos. And then came Christmas.

December 24, 1968, is arguably one of the more pivotal days in the history of civilization. For the first time since life was created, human beings escaped the pull and encumbrance of Earth's gravity and circled around another heavenly body, the Moon. It was Apollo 8, the mission that saved 1968—the mission that helped us see ourselves as we truly are.

On the fourth pass of the Moon, Frank Borman, James Lovell Jr., and William Anders became the first humans to behold the Earthrise. There, rising in the inky darkness of space like a beautiful blue Christmas ornament, was the Earth: every man, woman, and child; all the seas and mountains; the clouds and land masses; the animals and plants; all the knowledge, art, and literature; all the hate, love, tumult, and joy—everything rising, fragile and lonely; everything together in the vast expanse of the cosmos.

As the astronauts beamed this amazing image back to Earth, Anders said: "We are now approaching lunar sunrise and, for all the people back on Earth, the crew of Apollo 8 has a message that we would like to send to you."

Then each astronaut in turn read from the creation story in the book of Genesis, including, in part:

In the beginning God created the heaven and
    the earth....
And the Spirit of God moved upon the face of
    the waters.
And God said, Let there be light: and there was light....

And God said, Let there be a firmament in the midst
of the waters, and let it divide the waters from the
waters...and it was so....
And God called the dry land Earth; and the gathering
together of the waters called the Seas: and God saw
that it was good.

They concluded: "And from the crew of Apollo 8, we close with
good night, good luck, a Merry Christmas—and God bless all of
you, all of you on the good Earth."

It was 1968, and for the first time, we got to see ourselves
from that unique vantage point. We saw what God saw, and
we remembered that it was good. For it was on this beautiful,
fragile planet that God decided to make a home and took flesh
as a little child.

All these years later, there is still tumult, turmoil, and tur-
bulence on planet Earth. There is still war and want. It seems
that in many ways, we have forgotten the perspective of Apollo
8, where for the first time we could see ourselves as God sees
us: as one wonderfully diverse family, deeply connected and
incredibly good.

God took flesh on this precious planet as if to say, "Now do
you see how good you are? I have become who *you* are. In Jesus,
I will know what it is to be you. I will know what it is to dance
and to be afraid. I will know what it is like to touch someone's
face, to bury a loved one, to feel tears roll down my cheeks, to
be unable to stop laughing. I will know what it is to be you,
for I have become who you are so you might see that *who you
are is good*."

Every child on this planet needs to know they are good. Through words and in silence, they need to understand: "Your life matters. You are loved. You are important. You are beautiful." However we say that, however they see it in our eyes, feel it in our care, or touch it in our prayer, every child of any age needs to know: "You are good."

And you who read this book now? If you have not truly heard this before, please hear it now. God wants you to know this profound truth: "*You are good. You* are. In fact, you don't even know how good you are."

19

Forgiving Ourselves

*It is such a great moment of liberation
when you learn to forgive yourself,
let the burden go, and walk out into a
new path of promise and possibility.*

JOHN O'DONOHUE

Are there things you said or didn't say that bother you? Are there things you did or didn't do that you still think about, and which leave you with tightness in your shoulders or a sick feeling in the pit of your stomach?

Those of us who struggle with perfectionistic tendencies are more likely than most to continue to be so bothered. Sometimes it's things we've done that hurt someone or ourselves. Often, it's merely human foibles that are quite understandable to most people. But these things still bother us sometimes.

I get it. I still recall an ordination ceremony for new deacons years ago when I forgot the name of the pope right in front of the bishop and what seemed like a billion other people.

My question for you: What would you say to me about that? There were about twenty priests there, a bishop, about ten deacon candidates, and a church full of families and friends. When it was my turn during Mass to pray aloud for the pope, I drew a blank at his name. It was *quite* obvious. What is your reaction to me? How would you advise me to think and feel about that?

Also, I sometimes think of a missed opportunity from years ago when I was helping distribute Holy Communion and saw a woman in our parish who I knew to be in trouble. She was divorced from her husband, leaving several young children in his care. Earlier that week, someone told me she was living in her car. I hadn't seen her in a while, but now there she was in my Communion line. Though it is not something I would normally do, I thought maybe God would have me squeeze her hand or do something like that to let her know how glad we were that she was with us. But when it was her turn and she stepped in front of me, I waited too long and missed my chance.

What would you say to me about that? To this day, I think God was nudging me in that moment to do my part to help her know that she still mattered to us, that she belonged. Since I was the pastor, I think it would have meant a lot coming from me. But for whatever reason, I did nothing. Honestly, I think I felt self-conscious. Would you be compassionate to me about that?

Whether or not you are, I know I am called to be compassionate to myself about those things. I want to learn from my missed opportunities. But God does not want me to live my days regretting my foibles and my failures.

If you *are* able to be compassionate to me about those things, can you also be merciful to yourself? Once Jesus told his followers that when they inevitably experienced failure or rejection, they were to then "shake the dust" from their feet (Matthew 10:14) and move on.

We humans are finite and fallible. Failure happens. We mess up in ways big and small. Plans fall apart. Relationships end. Business ventures fail. Our body struggles. So does our mental health. Dreams don't materialize. We would do well to not be so surprised when these things happen.

God would have us treat ourselves with compassion about all of that, remembering that in our common humanity we *all* flub up! It is good that we are aware of those pangs in the pits of our stomachs, but we are urged not to dwell on or over-identify with them.

God does not want us to let our mistakes and weaknesses haunt us. Instead, we are to acknowledge reality, learn what we can, make amends where possible, and then keep moving forward.

We can get so stuck in our remorse that we miss out on the joys of life. We can spend so much inner energy on self-recrimination that we miss new opportunities to do good when they are presented before us.

We are invited simply to move forward, to choose again to love. It's all we can do. It's all we need to do. *You and I are more than the sum of our failures and mistakes!*

In his book *Tattoos on the Heart,* the Jesuit priest Fr. Gregory Boyle quotes Anthony de Mello: "Behold the one beholding you, and smiling," he writes. "It is truly hard for us to see the truth that disapproval does not seem to be any part of God's DNA. God is just too busy loving us to have any time for disappointment."

You or I might be someone who can't seem to forget our past mistakes and failures. But God is not as interested in those as we are. Instead, God yearns to remind us that we are loved just as we are and then invites us to again choose to love ourselves and this world.

20

The Practice of Gratitude

*"Enjoy the little things, for one day
you may look back and realize
they were the big things."*

ROBERT BRAULT

From my vantage point as a priest, I see something at church each Thanksgiving Day that moves me. As I look out at the congregation, there are always people who have recently buried a loved one or suffered some other heartache or challenge. Still, they choose to come to give thanks to God. They often sing and pray through their tears.

What is it that would lead them to be there in the midst of their pain? Why would they come to give thanks to God, knowing that this will be their first Thanksgiving Day with an empty place at the table or dealing with some other loss?

Sometimes, I gently ask them. They reply, in varying ways, that they've learned it is important to be people who *practice* being thankful. They are right. The practice of gratitude is one of the most crucial habits for a meaningful, joy-filled life.

In life, the good and the bad certainly don't cancel each other out. We are imperfect and this world is imperfect. Sometimes, aspects of our lives are tedious or tiresome. And sometimes we face heartache and pain, burdens which seem impossible to bear. It is important that we mourn our losses in whatever forms our grief takes and cry as often and as long as it is in our hearts to do so.

Yet, as the folks who come to pray with broken hearts on Thanksgiving Day remind us, there are things to be grateful for in the midst of it all. There are still blessings woven into the losses and the letting go, the deadlines and discouragements of our daily lives. How fortunate we are when we are able to see those blessings. It's too easy to forget how blessed we are.

However we do it, practicing thankfulness is vital to our mental and spiritual health. A lack of gratitude is at the heart of much that ails our souls. The more we look for things to complain about, the more we will find them—because these things are there. It is so easy to become someone who does this a lot.

In the same way, the more we look for things for which to be grateful, the more we will find them—because they are also there. Even in the midst of what is painful about life, there are blessings to be found. And the more we recognize our blessings amid all that life throws at us, the more we become grateful people, and the more we will have a reservoir of resilience to draw upon when needed.

The best way—perhaps the *only* way—to become a grateful person is to *practice* gratitude.

One summer, my job was driving a tractor to help clear some fields. For reasons I don't remember now, I decided that each day I would spend the first fifteen minutes of my time on that tractor thinking of things for which to be grateful. The first day, after I had thought of everything I could think of to be thankful for, I looked at my watch and saw that only six minutes had elapsed.

But the more I practiced being grateful, the more I noticed things to be grateful for. After a few days, it became quite easy and natural to spend those fifteen minutes thanking God— often for different things each day. I was learning to see how truly blessed I was. To this day, each time I walk the sidewalk from the rectory where I live over to church or school, I try to pause inwardly to remember some of the blessings of the day so far. They are countless.

When author and speaker Patricia Livingston led a mission for a parish where I served, she shared that she had a sister who struggled with mental illness. For her sister, the world would become dark at times, and she would need inpatient care. Their phone conversations and visits were challenging. Pat developed the tradition of asking her, "What's one good thing?" And her sister could always find one good thing to be grateful for, even in the thick of the most difficult day. That changed the mood of their conversation; that changed Pat's sister. Again, the more we look for things for which to be grateful, the more we will find them.

Many have found great benefit in keeping a gratitude journal. I recommend it. Each day, using a word, phrase, or sentence, jot down three things for which you are grateful. The next day, jot down three different things, and again the next day. Many do this for a month, and some even for a lifetime.

At the end of this book, in Appendix C "Practicing Gratitude," I offer a guided meditation that you might find of value.

I will invite you to picture someone you love who is living or who has died and imagine offering your thanks to them in any way you feel drawn to do so.

If you do not yet have a regular way to practice thankfulness and you eventually choose one, I imagine the practice itself will become one of the things for which you will become truly grateful. To practice gratitude changes us.

21

A Closing Word

Dear Human:

You've got it all wrong.

You didn't come here
to master unconditional love.
This is where you came from
and where you'll return.

You came here to learn personal love.
Universal love.
Messy love.
Sweaty love.
Crazy love.
Broken love.
Whole love.
Infused with divinity.
Lived through the grace of stumbling...

COURTNEY A. WALSH

When children come forward during Communion who are not yet old enough to receive the Sacrament, I give them a simple blessing. Once, when six-year-old Brady came forward with his mom, I offered him the blessing I use most often: "May you grow up to be like Jesus," I said. Immediately, Brady stepped back, gave a thumbs up and a big smile, and said, "Thanks. You, too!" I still laugh at that, but that *is* my goal.

At this time in my life, I serve primarily as the full-time pastor of a growing parish. When I can, I also try to find time to write books for kids or adults. As you might imagine, given my perfectionistic energies, right now I strongly wish I had more time to continue to review and edit what I have written. (Note to self: Trying to write a book about perfectionism while being a perfectionist is not for the faint of heart.)

But the work and research I've done in the process has itself helped me become more alive and free. And so I say—albeit somewhat timidly—*this book is good enough just as it is.* I put that sentence in writing for you so it might help you do the same with various efforts in your life. I also put that sentence in writing to hear myself saying it, to help me let go a bit.

This book is good enough—and so are you. If you struggle to believe this is true, I will believe it for you. Until you can catch up inwardly to believe that you are truly good enough just as you are, I'll believe it for you. You might find it hard to accept that it's true. I *know* it is true.

Since it is sometimes difficult for many of us to feel at peace, to trust that we already have what we need inside, that we are wanted and loved just as we are, here is a four-line reflection you might want to say from time to time.

My recommendation is that you say the first line, then pause to let that sink in a bit. Then say the first two lines together, pausing again at the end. Then say the first three lines together followed by a pause. Then, finally, say all four.

If you don't want to do this, it's OK, of course. You are already a person of deep-down goodness just as you are. In any case, here are the four lines I invite you to say one at a time:

I don't have to try so hard.

I am loved

just as I am,

more than I could ever know.

What I say to you with all my heart and with every fiber of my being is this: You *don't* have to try so hard. You *are* loved just as you are, more than you could ever know.

APPENDICES

THE WORRIES AND QUESTIONS OF CHILDREN

Grown-ups and adolescents aren't the only ones who struggle with perfectionism. Children of all ages wrestle with anxiety and questions about self-worth. Environment and trauma greatly affect a child's likelihood of struggling with perfectionistic tendencies. Some kids are shy, others more outgoing, but many struggle with anxiety of one type or another.

There are wonderful resources to help children and the adults who love them. I thank all of you who work so generously to love the children of the world in *any* of the ways you do.

Each quarter I write an article called "Ask Father Joe" for a little booklet called *Living Faith Kids*. Children (or their parents) submit questions, and I give short reflections in response.

Recent questions from Aisha and Brendan show how children may struggle with perfectionism from an early age, in ways that are often similar to how we may struggle as adults. It's good that we are aware that children also struggle. In the hope that you might find something of value, those two articles prompted by Aisha's and Brendan's questions are reproduced below. May God help us love well the children entrusted to our care. May God help each of us love the child in our own hearts.

* * * * *

Dear Father Joe,
How do I know how hard to try?
I get so nervous sometimes.
Aisha

Dear Aisha,

Sometimes I get pretty nervous, too. Yes, it's good that I try my best, that I work hard on things that are important. For example, before I preach at Mass on Sundays, I spend many hours preparing, and work really, really hard to do the best I can, because I think it is just so important. Sometimes in my life, however, I try too hard and worry a bit too much. It sounds like you might do that also.

There are some things to think about that can help us not be so nervous. It might be good, for example, to occasionally remind yourself of some of your good qualities. Perhaps it's good to keep in mind that no one is perfect, that everyone messes up, that everyone struggles sometimes. It's OK to struggle! Or you might do well to think about some of the times you are the happiest and to remember how that feels inside.

In any case, Aisha, these things are true: You have nothing to prove. It's OK if you make mistakes. (Everyone does.) And there is nothing you have to earn. You see, you are loved, just as you are. You are! You don't have enough power to make God stop loving you. You don't.

Perhaps you might want to find a way to keep these words as a reminder and to say them to yourself from time to time, pausing after each line:

I don't have to try so hard.
I am loved
just as I am,
more than I could ever know.

In Christ,
Fr. Joe

*   *   *   *   *

Dear Father Joe,
Is it hard to get to heaven? (Mom said Grandma
is there, but I don't know if I'll make it.)
Brendan

Dear Brendan,
If I could, I would love to help you not worry about whether you'll get to heaven. One thing I know is that God loves you just as you are, and that God wants you—and all of us—to one day be with God in heaven! Please know that God does not make it hard to get there.

The path to heaven is to be loving and kind. That, of course, is sometimes hard to do. But God does not expect us to be perfect. God just wants us to keep trying and, when we mess up, to be willing to begin again with God's help.

You see, heaven is filled with imperfect people. Everyone in heaven is far from perfect, someone who just kept trying. If we want to be good people, and if we try to be loving and kind during the days we have on earth, we don't have to worry about getting to heaven.

Even now, I imagine that God hears your grandma's prayers for you. I'm sure that your grandma—who knows how wonderful and loving God is—would also tell you not to worry. You just be you and love this world in your own way. And one day, you will again be with your grandma. And you will together be with the God who always loved you and who always will.

In Christ,
Fr. Joe

GUIDED MEDITATION: OUR BODIES, BROKEN AND BELOVED

A mother told me about a very diplomatic young man who came to pick up her daughter for a date. Because of a misunderstanding, he arrived an hour before her daughter expected. The daughter was just starting to get ready, didn't know it was he, and answered the door with her hair going in six million directions. She tried to make light of the awkward moment by saying, "How do you like my hair?" He stood there for a second and said—and I love this: "It looks like it's about to become something wonderful."

Great answer, young man. It's good to point out that, whatever her hair looked like in the moment, it already *was* something wonderful.

There is something about our bodies, just as they are, that deserves our awe. Our imperfect, wounded bodies are a marvel, lots of work, a source of embarrassment and shame, a gift beyond measure, something we will one day leave behind in this form, and a wonderful blessing worthy of our love and tenderness. Our bodies hold who we are and allow us to live in this world. And our bodies matter to God.

Whatever we may think of our bodies, the truth is that God loves us and the bodies we have just as they are. God wants us to *also* have tenderness and compassion for our bodies.

In a moment, I will invite you to use your imagination and to bring your body, just as it is, to God. Though some use imagery more readily than others, I encourage you to try it.

For prayer, I always think it is good to find a posture that keeps us both comfortable and alert. I encourage you to place yourself in that posture now. Please don't be limited by what I suggest. If your imagination takes you elsewhere, relax into that. At one point I will suggest words that God might have for you. Please listen to what God has for you through these words—or in spite of them. If it helps to have music in the background or someone else slowly read the words while you listen, I encourage that.

This process is meant to be experienced slowly, with pauses throughout. As you bring your body to God, you can use words, or you can let there be no words.

When using imagery in prayer, some find it helps to first take a few deep breaths. Many choose to breathe in through the nose and out through the mouth. Try that now. As you do so, become aware of having a body...of being alive...of being you.

In your imagination, whether or not you see Jesus, sense his presence with you. Hear him say your name. Then listen to Jesus say:

> *I had a body once—an earthly body like yours. It wasn't meant to last forever. But I found blessings in having one. Your body is a blessing, too. I invite you to be grateful for the body you have.*

You pause for a moment to let that sink in. Can you be grateful for having a body? Is there anything you would thank God for about having a body? If so, bring that to God now in any way you like. With gestures, words, or just by your awareness, open up to God anything for which you are grateful about your body. When it is time, Jesus speaks again:

> *Tell me of those things you don't like about your body and where it hurts to be you.*

Go ahead. What would you like to say to Jesus about those parts of your body that you don't like—those places where you are in pain, feel embarrassed, or think you are diminished? With or without words, tell Jesus about it. Let him know what your body is like for you. After you have done so, and when you are ready, listen to Jesus' response as he says to you:

> *I want you to hear me when I say, "I love you as you are." You are, of course, so much more than the gifts of your body, and so much more than its wounds or imperfections. Whatever you think and feel about*

your body now, please know that I love you just as you are. I do. And I will be with you always and forever. Always I will be with you, loving you.

Now again become aware of being in the place you are. Notice what it sounds, smells, feels, or looks like to be there. As you do so, try to keep a sense of the presence of God with you.

Of course, some people find it easier than others to use their imaginations in this way. If that was helpful for you, I'm glad. If not, or if you fell asleep, that's OK. It is still true that your body, broken and beloved, is important and worthy of being treasured. And God truly does love you just as you are.

GUIDED
MEDITATION:
PRACTICING
GRATITUDE

A woman once described her grandfather as a person who truly understood what mattered. She recounted the Thanksgiving meal when her grandpa and younger brother were the ones chosen to participate in their family Thanksgiving post-dinner custom. Each year, two family members would make a wish and then together break the turkey wishbone. The person who ended up with the longer part was the one who was supposed to have a wish come true. Little brother was excited about his wish and really wanted to win. He was, of course, crestfallen when he ended up with the smaller portion of the bone. "That's all right," said Grandpa with his kind smile. "My wish was that you would get yours."

As I mentioned earlier in the book, I am always moved on Thanksgiving Day to see the number of people who come to give thanks to God even in the midst of heartache or loss. It strikes me that I do not need to say much that day. On one level, like that grandfather, those folks already understand what really matters and the importance of giving thanks.

Perhaps their presence is so striking to me because it is so easy for each of us to forget just how blessed we are. Because life is so hectic, we sometimes miss the countless blessings woven into an ordinary day. Because we are so rushed, we often live on the surface of things. With so much tugging at our attention, we often aren't fully awake to what is truly important.

Perhaps some version of this prayer activity might be helpful. I will simply offer several questions followed by some time to think, reflect, and use our imaginations.

As with the previous guided reflection, I encourage you to find a posture that helps you be alert, yet comfortable. If it helps to have soft music playing in the background or someone else slowly reading the words while you listen, please do so:

1. First, take a few deep breaths. Many choose to breathe in through the nose and out through the mouth. As you breathe deeply in and out, become aware of having a body...of being alive...of being you.

2. Picture yourself somewhere you like to be that is comfortable and safe. In your imagination, settle comfortably into your spot and enjoy its peace for a few seconds. You might notice what it smells, feels, looks, or sounds like to be there.

3. Next, I invite you to imagine saying a word of thanks to someone you know. There will be pauses to think

about whom you'd choose and what you'd want to say. Please go at your own pace and only as you feel drawn to participate. The person to whom you offer thanks could be someone living or someone who has died. Who pops up in your mind or heart to choose? A parent, teacher, or friend? Who? If you had a chance to say thank you to someone you know, who would you thank?

4. When you think of someone, what would you thank them for? Maybe they believed in you, taught you something important, or welcomed you back. Perhaps they nurtured you, inspired you, sacrificed for you. Or what?

5. Now picture yourself in that safe place and let yourself sense the presence of that person with you. In time, offer your thanks. With or without words, say what you want to say to that person.

6. When you have finished, do you sense there is something that person wants to say to you? Let the person say something to you now. What do they say?

7. Is there anything else you would like to say in response? Go ahead and do so.

8. Now it's time to say farewell. If you like, in your imagination you can take that person's hand, give

them a hug, or say goodbye however it is in your heart to do so.

9. Finally, when you are ready, become aware again of being bodily in the place you are and try to keep a sense of God's presence with you as you do so.

Of course, some people find it easier than others to use their imagination in this way. If you found blessing in that meditation, I'm glad. If not, that's OK. If that was difficult, or you fell asleep, it is still true that we have many reasons and people for which to be profoundly grateful.

In any case, in a little while, you will close this book and return to whatever life has for you next. Whatever mixture the rest of this day holds, isn't it true that we also have much for which to be grateful? Aren't we blessed beyond measure?

Wouldn't it be good if, by the grace of God, we were able to go through this day, and each day, just a little more awake to what really matters—to what we really value?

As best we can, let us hold on to the imperfect, precious, simple, mixed, messy, ordinary moments of our lives. They hold us. They hold love. They hold God.